BLACKBURN WITH DARWEN LI

D0313637

Mind Maps®
in a week

**STEVE MORRIS AND
JANE SMITH**

**Edited by
CHRIS BAKER**

Hodder & Stoughton

A MEMBER OF THE HODDER HEADLINE GROUP

Acknowledgement

The authors would like to thank Vanda North,
Director of Buzan Centres, for her valuable comments
and feedback while they were writing this book.

Mind Maps are a Registered Trade Mark of the Buzan
Organisation, used with permission and enthusiasm.

011842020

Orders: please contact Bookpoint Ltd, 39 Milton Park, Abingdon, Oxon OX14
4TD. Telephone: (44) 01235 827720, Fax: (44) 01235 400454. Lines are open from
9.00–6.00, Monday to Saturday, with a 24 hour message answering service.
Email address: orders@bookpoint.co.uk

British Library Cataloguing in Publication Data
A catalogue record for this title is available from The British Library

ISBN 0 340 84952 5

First published 1998
Impression number   10   9   8   7   6   5   4   3   2   1
Year   2007   2006   2005   2004   2003   2002

Copyright © 1998, 2002 Jane Smith, Steve Morris

All rights reserved. No part of this publication may be reproduced or
transmitted in any form or by any means, electronic or mechanical, including
photocopy, recording, or any information storage and retrieval system,
without permission in writing from the publisher or under licence from the
Copyright Licensing Agency Limited. Further details of such licences (for
reprographic reproduction) may be obtained from the Copyright Licensing
Agency Limited, of 90 Tottenham Court Road, London W1P 9HE.

Typeset by SX Composing DTP, Rayleigh, Essex
Printed in Great Britain for Hodder & Stoughton Educational, a division of
Hodder Headline Plc, 338 Euston Road, London NW1 3BH by Cox and
Wyman, Reading, Berkshire.

chartered
management
institute

inspiring leaders

The leading organisation for professional management

As the champion of management, the Chartered Management Institute shapes and supports the managers of tomorrow. By sharing intelligent insights and setting standards in management development, the Institute helps to deliver results in a dynamic world.

Setting and raising standards

The Institute is a nationally accredited organisation, responsible for setting standards in management and recognising excellence through the award of professional qualifications.

Encouraging development, improving performance

The Institute has a vast range of development programmes, qualifications, information resources and career guidance to help managers and their organisations meet new challenges in a fast-changing environment.

Shaping opinion

With in-depth research and regular policy surveys of its 91,000 individual members and 520 corporate members, the Chartered Management Institute has a deep understanding of the key issues. Its view is informed, intelligent and respected.

For more information call 01536 204222 or visit www.managers.org.uk

■■■■ C O N T E N T S ■■■■

Fortune Magazine trumpets from its front cover that brain power is the best way to make a fortune.

The South East Asian Economic Review trumpets from its front cover that brain power is 'where it's at' and that the labour shortage puts Asia's economic boom at risk. The first time in history that 'labour' has been used to mean not muscle power, but brain power.

Skandia, the multi-national insurance giant based in Stockholm, changed its standard annual report format to include a major supplement entitled *Intellectual Capital* – an accounting for the 'intellectual power' of its company and its customers.

The Brain Trust Charity, an international charity devoted to intelligence, recently declared the 21st century to be the 'Century of the Brain' and the coming millennium to be the 'Millennium of the Mind'.

In view of the exponentially new information on the brain and its functions, it is essential that we have a thinking tool that allows us to use the brain's extraordinary powers. That thinking tool is the Mind Map.

The Mind Map is a multi-dimensional piece of thinking equipment that allows the individual to use all the 'fingers of intelligence' – in other words all the multiple intelligences. The Mind Map has been described as 'the Swiss army knife for the brain'. Since its first-form discovery in the late 1960s, the Mind Map has been used increasingly by the international community. At the time of the first edition of *Mind Maps® in a Week,* most of the *Fortune 500* companies have used this thinking technique with increasing and accelerating frequency. To name just a few of those Mind Mapping: American Express, AT & T,

■ FOREWORD BY TONY BUZAN ■

Barclays International, Boeing, BP, British Airways, British Telecom, EDS, Encyclopaedia Britannica, Ernst & Young, General Motors, Goldman Sachs, IBM, Institute for Management Studies, Microsoft, National Westminister Bank plc, Rank Xerox, Walt Disney, etc.

Specifically, IBM is using Mind Mapping at their accounting headquarters in New York to handle all their major accounting processes. Tony Dottino, their trainer, estimates that they have saved tens of millions of dollars by using the Mind Map thinking process. Dr. Michael Stanley, the head of a 100-plus strong engineering division devoted to the making of aircraft, recently won the Boeing Quality Award for saving his company over 12 million dollars in nine months by using Mind Mapping as the primary communication technique in the development of the aircraft. The Liechtenstein Global Trust, a 110 billion dollar holding bank and finance institution uses Mind Maps throughout the organisation, especially in the context of its Renaissance Academy, a revolutionary new training programme based on both the Greek and the Italian Renaissance.

In this introductory book *Mind Maps® in a Week*, contributed to by Vanda North, the top international trainer of Mind Map trainers, the authors Steve Morris and Jane Smith take you through the theory and development of Mind Maps, and through the innumerable business uses to which they can be applied.

With this book you will learn how to manage your mind and you will be investing in the most important currency of all, which is not the yen, not the dollar, not the franc, not the pound – it is the currency of intelligence. You will be investing in your Intellectual Capital!

The central aim of this book is to help you to understand the art and science of Mind Mapping. Once you have learned this skill, you will be able to organise your thoughts better, tap into your creative energies and improve your memory.

A Mind Map is a tool that mirrors the way in which the brain stores and retrieves information. It is a powerful way of expressing the thought patterns, pictures and associations that already exist in the brain.

Mind Maps were developed by Tony Buzan to help people to understand the brain and to harness its creative power. The brain is a 'sleeping giant': its power and versatility surpass that of any man-made computer. But most people only use about 1% of its full capacity.

Mind Maps are not a simple panacea for every problem and every situation. It takes time to develop the required skills and to find out how they can work for you. Nevertheless, when you begin to put the techniques we describe into practice, you will begin to notice changes in every part of your life. For example:

- you will understand and absorb information more easily
- you will be able to recall information quickly
- your decisions will be more effective
- you will feel more relaxed and in control of your time
- your creativity will be enhanced

We hope that Mind Mapping will help you to learn how to learn, to develop your skills and ultimately to achieve your true potential.

Why you need Mind Mapping

With the world as competitive as it is, the ability to process information can be the difference between success and failure. This is not easy when you consider the vast amount of information and knowledge that we need to arm ourselves with.

However, the real problem is not knowing things, but to continue knowing things. The current estimate says that to stay on top of our jobs, we will need to re-educate ourselves every 3 years.

For many, Mind Mapping has proved to be an invaluable tool in the process. It is a simple technique, but can have far-reaching benefits for those who master it. It can help us all to assimilate masses of information and, crucially, know how to relate each bit to all the others.

Much more than that, it can help boost self-confidence in your own ability and improve the way you feel about

yourself. Being able to call to mind a piece of critical and interesting information to illustrate your point can make you a better speaker and improve presentations that you have to give to clients.

But what exactly are Mind Maps? How were they discovered and the technique developed? And, most importantly, how can they help you in your everyday life? Our task for Sunday is to answer these questions.

Buzan's great invention

Mind Mapping emerged as a result of Tony Buzan's research into areas such as psychology, the neurophysiology of the brain, science, memory, mnemonics and creative thinking. He concluded that lengthy written notes can actually act as a barrier to learning. What was needed was a technique that actually mirrors the way that the brain stores and retrieves information.

As a teacher, Buzan began to develop his theory of learning and the techniques of Mind Mapping by encouraging his pupils to work with key words and pictures rather than lines of writing. He realised that many pupils who had been identified as 'backward', 'hopeless' or 'unteachable' were actually very bright. When they were given the tools with which to learn and express themselves, they soon progressed by leaps and bounds. From this experience, he concluded that it's not just the so-called underachievers who are being failed by the current system. Many (if not most) people never manage to make the most of their natural abilities. This is not because they lack the resources to learn but simply because they have never been told how to use those resources.

In 1974, Buzan published his book on Mind Mapping, *Use Your Head*. He aimed to introduce Mind Maps to at least 10 per cent of the world's population by the year 2000. This book is our contribution towards achieving that goal.

Your own experience

Most people, no matter how successful they are in later life, can recount some experience at school, college or university that has had a negative effect on their self-image, their motivation or their ability to learn.

Activity

Have you ever underachieved as a result of not knowing how to learn? Make a note of your own experience.

We don't intend this exercise to sound like a criticism of teachers – they have always worked within the boundaries of their own knowledge about learning, motivation and the brain. It's important to remember that:

- the actual location of the brain was only discovered 500 years ago
- the main thrust of research into the physiology and functioning of the brain has only been carried out in the last 150 years
- some of the most important discoveries about the different mental areas and the potential patterns that the brain can make were only made during the late 1960s and early 1970s

Brain research is one of the last great frontiers of science, and now, in the 1990s, it seems that each month yet more new and amazing discoveries are being made. Scientists are sure of one thing: we still know less than 1 per cent of what there is to know about the workings and the capacity of the human brain.

Despite the immense body of knowledge that is now being accumulated about the brain's fantastic powers, few people know how to make the best use of what nature has given them. As school pupils, hardly any of us were taught how to think, remember, analyse and learn. Although we were all taught how to read, we were not told how the eye works during the process of reading. Although we were told to concentrate, we were not taught how to focus our attention and use our time to best advantage. And although we were told to make notes, we were not given any help in making notes in a form that the brain can process easily.

Your mind: a computer

One of the reasons why human beings find it difficult to study the nature of learning is that they are actually living inside the object that they want to know more about – the brain itself.

A good way to gain a more objective appreciation of the brain's potential is to think of it as a very small, enormously complex and tremendously powerful computer. In fact, no computer that has yet been invented is capable of doing what the brain can do. The brain can think logically and creatively at the same time, it can conjure up images in its mind's eye, it can think the body warm or cool, it can make itself healthy or ill. Everything we are or do – consciously or unconsciously – starts off as a picture or an idea inside the brain. Even if we were able to build a computer that could do all these things, it would weigh more than 10 tons and would need to be housed inside a building as large as the Albert Hall.

Like all computers, however, your brain is only as efficient as the way it is programmed and used. To get the best out of your brain/computer, you need to:

- *programme it correctly* – give it a goal, a purpose, a focus, even a challenge. Brains work much better if they know what they are being asked to achieve
- *feed in the right data* – the more information you feed in, the better it will work. You can get the information you need from an infinite number of sources in the world around you
- *process the data effectively* – Mind Maps are a great way of getting your data organised so that you know exactly how they are contributing towards achieving your goals
- *maintain it effectively* – this means eating a sensible diet, taking an adequate amount of exercise and avoiding poisoning your system (too often!)

What is a Mind Map?

It seems that everyone who uses Mind Maps has their own way of describing what they are. Here are a few of the typical things people say about them:

- 'a way of hot-wiring your creative energies'
- 'a multi-handed thought-ball catcher'
- 'a way of catching, organising and interpreting thoughts and ideas'
- 'putting on paper what's in your head'
- 'doodling with a purpose'

Before we go much further, you may find it useful to see an example of a Mind Map. Here is an example of one that was created as a plan of this section of the current book.

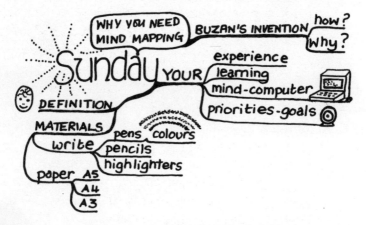

Figure 1 *A Mind Map for Sunday*

A Mind Map is a powerful way of expressing the thought patterns, pictures and associations that already exist in the brain. As you can see in the diagram, the principal thought or idea is drawn in the centre of a blank page, with major branches, representing connected themes, radiating out from the centre. Second and third levels of thought, expressed in terms of key words or images, are connected to the main branches with thinner lines.

You will see many more examples of Mind Maps as you read on through the book, and you will soon start to create some of your own. For the moment, it is enough just to note some of the main features of a Mind Map:

- *it is visual:* this is important because the mind thinks in images, rather than in words. Pictures are a powerful means of expressing ideas, describing past events and making hopes materialise
- *it contains key words:* part of the information on a Mind Map is distilled down into a series of key words which themselves trigger images and other thoughts. The shape and resonances of the selected words add to the overall effectiveness of the Mind Map
- *the structure is based on associations:* a Mind Map allows the user to put together words and pictures that are closely associated, thus following the natural logic of the brain. This reinforces the memory, helps the user to think creatively and results in the clustering of ideas into separate themes

Much of the value of a Mind Map stems from the conscious involvement of the creator as it is being drawn. People become completely engrossed while they are creating their

Mind Maps, they enjoy the experience, and they derive a tremendous amount of satisfaction from doing it: all these factors add to the usefulness and effectiveness of the finished product.

What are your priorities?

The fact that you have picked up this book probably means that you would like to be able to develop some aspects of your mental skills. You may have experienced problems in the past or simply feel that, for some reason, you are not doing as well as you would like to. Remember that most people use only about 1 per cent of their full capacity, so there is plenty of room for improvement for all of us!

This next activity is an opportunity for you to clarify which areas you would most like to work on both while you are reading this book and as a follow-up to this week's study.

Activity

Note down on a piece of paper up to six 'mental functions' that you would like to improve (e.g. memory, ability to concentrate).

Mind Mapping can help you to use your brain in the way it was meant to be used. In doing this, you can overcome a variety of problems:

- difficulty in recalling people's names
- poor memory in a more general sense
- a lack of concentration
- feeling overwhelmed by mountains of information

- a fear of public speaking
- difficulty in thinking creatively
- time-management problems
- uncertainty about decision-making or problem-solving
- finding it difficult to prioritise
- difficulty in organising thoughts effectively

Recognising the areas that you want to concentrate on is the first important step in getting more out of your brain and out of your life. Now try translating your problems into goals and writing them along the lines of the mini Mind Map shown in the diagram. We've also put in an example to show you how you might do this.

Figure 2   *'Mini' Mind Map goals*

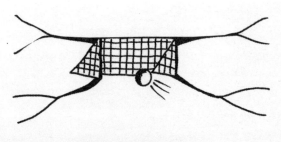

Figure 3   *Your goals*

What materials do you need?

To become a Mind Mapper, you will need certain materials:

- a set of felt-tip pens – it's a good idea to have some thin ones for writing and drawing and thicker ones for 'colouring in'
- some good-quality plain white paper – both A4 and A3 size. You can buy artists pads or, when you become really enthusiastic, Mind Mapping pads from the Buzan Centre.

It's also nice to have:

- some soft drawing pencils
- a set of highlighters

Don't worry if you haven't got any of these things at the moment. You can do a lot with just two or three colours in the beginning. But when you become more absorbed in Mind Mapping, you will want to have good materials readily available.

Summary

Today, you have been introduced to the idea of Mind Mapping and its assumption that the mind contains immense untapped potential. You have considered the key features of Mind Maps and how these can help to improve your mental performance, once you have prioritised areas you wish to work on.

Not one brain but two!

Today and tomorrow, you will be learning a few basic facts about the brain that will help you to understand why Mind Maps are constructed in the way that they are.

Although Mind Mapping is a very practical everyday skill, you do need to get inside the thinking that led to its development. Today is part of that process.

Two brains – two kinds of skills

Seen from above, the cortex (or outer part) of the human brain looks just like the two halves of a walnut. These left and right 'hemispheres' are joined in the centre by a thick nerve cable called the 'corpus callosum'. You probably already know that the two sides of the body are connected to the brain in a cross-over fashion. This is why the left side of the body is affected if the right side of the brain is damaged, and vice versa.

Very little was known about the functions of the two hemispheres for hundreds of years, except that the left half of the brain seemed to control the speech and language functions and the right half seemed be more concerned with visual functions and judging distances. Because damage to the left side led to far more serious problems than damage to the right side, it was thought for a long time that the left side was the dominant hemisphere and the right side was the subordinate one.

Then, in the 1960s, Dr Roger Sperry, a scientist working in California, made some amazing new discoveries about the brain. He and his team found that the right side of the brain, far from being less important than the left side, simply gathers and processes information in a different way. A series of ingenious tests on 'split-brain' patients (people whose corpus callosums had been severed to control epileptic fits) revealed that each half of the brain specialises in different modes of thinking.

- the left side is good at putting ideas into words. It also analyses, counts and uses reason to draw conclusions. This side houses the rational mind – the part that loves order and sequence
- the right side is not quite so concerned with words. It sees things in terms of colourful 'mind's eye' pictures, metaphors and symbols. This is the intuitive side that creates and responds to music, movement and dreams, and that see the 'whole picture'

The diagram shown summarises the skills and concepts that are associated with each side of the brain.

The picture that we get is that the left side is all about maths, order and logic while the right side is about art, music and intuition. But, of course, it's not quite as simple as that. More recent brain research has discovered that each hemisphere is actually capable of performing many of the other one's functions. If the side that specialises in a particular set of skills shuts down for any reason, the other side is able to compensate to a certain extent.

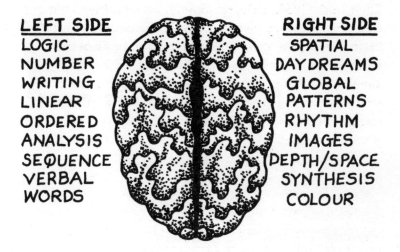

LEFT SIDE
LOGIC
NUMBER
WRITING
LINEAR
ORDERED
ANALYSIS
SEQUENCE
VERBAL
WORDS

RIGHT SIDE
SPATIAL
DAYDREAMS
GLOBAL
PATTERNS
RHYTHM
IMAGES
DEPTH/SPACE
SYNTHESIS
COLOUR

Figure 4   *Left- and right- brain areas of specialisation*

Tapping into our potential
Sperry proved that inside each of our heads we have two
hemispheres of the brain with two quite different approaches
to thinking, learning, knowing and expressing ideas. Our
brains are built to operate with both sides working in
harmony, each one complementing what the other half can
do. This is the perfect partnership. One side uses its
specialist skills to process information in a certain way and
then passes this over to the other side for further processing,
analysis or synthesis. So each side contributes different kinds
of skills to share the load and increase overall efficiency.

You can be a genius too!
Sometimes you hear people excusing their personal dislike of
creative approaches by saying that they are 'left-brained'.

Others may say that they trust their intuition rather than their logic because they are 'right-brained'. However, the research indicates that if people are talented in certain areas rather than others, this does not mean that they were born like it and have to stay that way. It simply means that one half of the brain is more highly developed than the other at the moment.

To achieve your full potential, it is important to use and develop both sides of your brain equally. Like most adults in Western society, this probably means taking steps to bring your right brain up to the same level of ability as the left side. Developing and using the skills of Mind Mapping will contribute significantly to the burgeoning of your right-brain functions.

If you read about talented or successful people throughout history, it soon becomes clear that they are ones who (consciously or unconsciously) made equal use of both parts of their brains. Leonardo da Vinci is an obvious example. This man was simultaneously an acclaimed painter and sculptor, an accomplished musician and composer, and a

great scientist and inventor. Another good example is Einstein who, far from spending his whole time working on complex mathematical equations, first initiated these by daydreaming, and also enjoyed playing the violin and sailing.

What is clear is that, if you concentrate on developing a mental area that you consider to be weak, you do not risk allowing your more highly developed skills to decline. On the contrary, working on your right-brain skills will have the effect of improving your left-brain skills as well.

How we lost the right-brain skills
Although the left side is not more important than the right, the skills associated with that side tend to be valued more – both in education and in business. The emphasis on logical analysis rather than creativity and intuition, means that many people have failed to develop their crucial right-brain skills. In fact, our highly sophisticated, verbal, technological culture denies many people access to their intuitive, imaginative powers.

Many of us have been through an education process which did not appreciate the importance of the right-brain skills. The right hemisphere, the daydreamer, the artist, the dancer, the intuitive child, were all lost in our school system. There may have been a few art classes, some creative writing, perhaps a chance to improvise music or dance. But the skills that were really valued, the ones that got you through exams and into college or university, were the ones that are associated with the left brain.

Take a little time to think through whether the left side of your brain is dominant.

Left-brain dominance
The dominance of the left side of the brain and the resulting subordination of the right is deeply ingrained in many cultures and in languages. Throughout human history, terms with connotations of good for the right hand (connected to the left hemisphere) and bad for the left hand (connected to the right hemisphere) have made an appearance in most languages. For example, the Latin word for left is *sinister* – meaning 'ominous', and the Latin word for right is *dexter* – from which we get our word 'dexterity', meaning skilful.

Because of the way we are, our whole lives and personalities are framed, encapsulated and defined by the words we use to describe ourselves. The problem is, though, that the right-brain skills are then left to chance. Mind Mapping argues that these other skills are too important for that, and that we have the opportunity to consciously gain access to them so that they may work together with left-brain skills, as initially intended.

What does this really have to do with Mind Mapping?

Hopefully, you are now starting to see how what we know about the two sides of the brain connects with our central theme of Mind Mapping. Mind Maps are constructed in such a way that they make use of the whole brain. This is the exact opposite to most forms of note-taking which tend to rely solely on left-brain skills.

These are the aspects of Mind Maps that appeal to the left side of the brain:

- they are ordered and rational
- they allow analysis – the creator or reader can see how an idea can be broken down logically
- they use key words to express facts or concepts
- they allow the creator to think in terms of linked ideas
- they use lines
- they allow individual facts or ideas to be grouped
- they have a structure

These are the aspects of Mind Maps that appeal to the right side of the brain:

- they use colour and pictures
- they can incorporate perspective
- they allow the creator or the reader to see the whole picture
- they help the creator (and anyone else) to see the relationships between things
- they use symbols and metaphors
- they are fun to make and attractive to look at

In creating Mind Maps, you will delve deeply into those parts of your mind that are usually masked by the superficial details of day-to-day life and work. Mind Mapping will allow you to harness the special abilities of both the left and the right sides of your brain. As your intuitive, imagistic powers and your logical, analytical skills start to develop more fully, you may start to notice changes in other parts of your life. You may find that your memory improves, that your mind can grasp and analyse ideas faster or that you can think quickly of more creative solutions to problems. And who knows where these kinds of changes might lead you? Mind Maps can transform your life forever!

The importance of colour and pictures
The part of Mind Mapping that most newcomers find it hardest to come to terms with is the use of colour and pictures. Although this is understandable given the level of the conditioning that we discussed earlier, it is these features more than anything else that open up the valuable and powerful right-brain skills.

You know that you would gain more from looking at a graph or a bar chart than from ploughing through a 1,000-word report. A cartoon can often capture and communicate a point much more clearly and instantaneously than a long-winded explanation. And a company wanting to sell something is going to be more successful if it uses a striking visual image than it would be if it tries to write about its product.

Remember that pictures can also be symbolic: they are capable of carrying several levels of meaning at the same time. This point is particularly important in Mind Mapping. You can draw a stylised elephant's head to represent memory, a cloud to represent a dream, a rainbow to represent hopes or ambitions, and so on. As you become more involved in the fascinating art of Mind Maps, more symbols will suggest themselves to you.

Can't draw? Won't draw?
Some people say that Mind Maps are not for them because they can't draw. If you really believe you are one of these people, you should read a book called *Drawing on the Right Side of the Brain* by Betty Edwards (see the reading list at the end of this book). In this inspiring book, the author sets out to help people to improve their drawing skills – especially those who feel they have little or no talent for drawing. She gives many examples of individuals who have become very competent artists after just a few weeks' or months' practice. She says:

> *You will soon discover that drawing is a skill that can be learned by any normal person with average eyesight and average eye–hand co-ordination.*

But you don't have to achieve a high level of skill in drawing to create Mind Maps. If you are able to stop telling yourself that you can't draw, you will certainly surprise yourself after just a few days' practice. What's more, you will soon experience the sheer delight at being able to express ideas and facts in pictures rather than in words.

Here are some tips on how anyone – even those who find drawing quite daunting – can incorporate more pictorial elements into their Mind Maps:

- *use shapes* – anyone can draw stars, squares, triangles, rectangles, circles, flashes and so on. With a bit of practice, you can put different shapes together to make people, buildings or patterns
- *use symbols* – question marks, exclamation marks, mathematical symbols and the Greek alphabet are examples of symbols that you can use instead of words
- *use stick figures* – after a while, you will be able to get them running, dancing, waving flags, thinking, listening to music and sleeping. You can give them interesting hairstyles, dress them in colourful clothes and give them different shapes and sizes

- *make words or letters into pictures* – this is a most useful trick to use when you are first setting out on your Mind Mapping career. Sometimes you can make a word into a picture:

Sometimes, a letter or letters suggest a picture that is related to the whole word:

Activity

Practise expressing ideas in colour and images rather than in words. What pictures do you see as you read the following list of words? Try sketching your mind's-eye images on a piece of paper, using felt-tip pens and coloured biros. Relax and have some fun as you do this.

book	dog
family	city
meeting	idea
funny	why
telephone	money

Everyone's minds will conjure up different pictures and different associations, as you will see tomorrow.

Summary

Today, you have got into some of the important ideas behind Mind Mapping and started to work on brain activities that will be useful during the week.

Get well connected

Yesterday you learned that the brain has a left side and a right side. You also started to practise expressing ideas in pictures – an activity which will help to develop your right-brain skills, if, like most people, those functions are less well used than the left side.

Today, you are going to look at two further important facts about the brain:

- it has far greater potential than most people ever imagine
- it works by association

Mind Maps will help you to make fuller use of your brain's immense potential and to harness its associative powers to think, plan and remember effectively.

Ten billion brain cells

Agatha Christie's famous detective, Hercule Poirot, was very fond of using the 'little grey cells'. But exactly how many of these cells did he, and do we, actually have? The answer is a staggering ten billion. (That is ten thousand million to break it down into bite-sized chunks!)

You may find it easier to grasp this vast figure if you think of it in terms of the number of people that inhabit our planet or the number of stars in our Milky Way. Exploring the private universe inside our own head can be as challenging and just as rewarding as any mission into space. We can visit places we didn't know existed and discover talents we never knew we had.

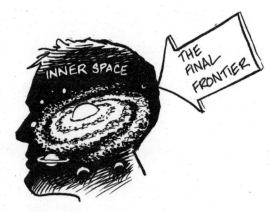

The capacity of the human brain is so vast that no-one has ever been able – and most probably, no-one will ever be able – to harness it completely. The fact is that the potential of human beings to take in and process information, to analyse facts and figures, to remember things, to integrate new learning with known facts, to think logically, to create new ideas, in short to turn their minds to anything they desire, is infinitely greater than most of us have ever imagined.

Know your neurons
Neurons are minute – millions would fit on a pin head. A typical neuron consists of a central body which has small fibres called dendrites growing out from it. These dendrites are like the branches of a tree, with smaller and smaller fibres sprouting from them like twigs. The main fibre – known as the axon – is longer and thicker than all the others. At the end of the axon, the fibre divides into yet more branches and twigs – see the diagram.

The main task of the dendrites is to receive data passed on from the axons of other brain cells.

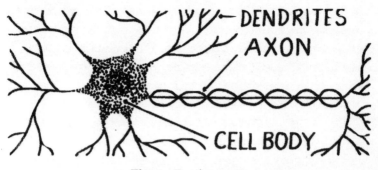

Figure 7 *A neuron*

This octopus-like structure is basically the same for all 10 billion neurons, although the number and size of the fibres vary widely in different parts of the brain:

- some have fewer than 10 dendrites on them, whereas others have hundreds or even thousands
- some dendrites and axons are minute, while others have fibres that are more than a metre in length – going from the brain right down to the base of the spinal cord

Making connections

Crammed together inside the brain, the 10 billion neurons encircle each other with their axon and dendrite tentacles. Sometimes, the axon touches the body of another brain cell, sometimes it connects with another dendrite. The place where two brain cells meet is called a synapse. When an electrical impulse travels from one brain cell to another, a chemical is transferred across the 'synaptic gap' between the two. This chemical creates another impulse that transfers the message on to the next brain cell and so on.

In the space of a microsecond, hundreds of electro-chemical impulses are spontaneously flashing across synaptic gaps in all directions inside your brain. What you have got inside your head is more complex and more powerful than any computer ever built. In fact, each tiny brain cell is powerful enough to receive and transmit hundreds of pieces of data every second. And in a split second, it is capable of processing data from several sources and sending them off along the appropriate pathways through the brain.

The facts about these pathways are even more mind-boggling than what we know about the neurons themselves. Every time you have a thought or an idea, a message is sent along a pathway that connects hundreds, thousands or hundreds of thousands of neurons. In the early 1970s, Professor Peter Anokhin of Moscow University published the results of 60 years of brain research. The main points that emerged from his work are as follows:

- each neuron can interact with between 1 and 100,000 neurons at any one time
- the number of different permutations that the 10 billion brain cells can make is so great that it would take a line of figures more than 10.5 million kilometres in length to describe it

This means that the patterns or maps of the mind that your brain is capable of making would stretch to the moon and back 14 times. So it is simply not true that a brain can become 'filled up to the top' and unable to learn anything new. In fact it can make an infinite number of memory traces, and the more connections it makes, the more connections it is able to make in the future.

There is little hope that scientists could ever analyse all these interconnections. It took a team of researchers three years just to look at the patterns made by a worm's brain – and this creature only has 23 neurons!

Paths through the jungle

At any one time, there may be hundreds of millions of impulses flashing around the brain, each one travelling along a known pathway or creating a new one. Scientists call these pathways 'memory traces', but they are easier to understand if you think of them as tracks through a dense forest. In *The Mind Map Book*, Tony Buzan notes:

> *Every time you have a thought the biochemical/ electromagnetic resistance is reduced. It is like trying to clear a path through a forest. The first time is a struggle because you have to fight your way through the undergrowth. The second time you travel that way will be easier because of the clearing you did in your first journey. The more times you travel that path, the less resistance there will be, until, after many repetitions, you have a wide smooth track which requires little or no clearing.*

The same thing happens in the brain when you are trying to learn something or develop a new skill. What you have to do is to clear a pathway by getting to grips with the idea or practising the skill for the first time. Then, by repeating the activity or revising the new information or ideas several times over, you will make a strong memory trace in your

brain that will allow quick recall or mastery of the desired skill.

Do brain cells die off?
If you lose something or forget to do something, the chances are that you explain the lapse by saying 'How could I do that? I must be getting old!' or 'Oh God, my brain cells are dying off!'.

But the truth is that:

- people of all ages forget things – even small children and teenagers who ought to be at the height of their mental powers
- there is little or no evidence to prove that neurons do die as people become older

All the evidence now seems to indicate that brain cells don't become fewer as we get older. On the contrary, the brain should become more effective with aging because its 'computer memory board' of thought patterns is bigger.

What happens as people age is that they start to accept the myth that their abilities have deteriorated and will go on doing so. This belief soon becomes self-fulfilling and self-perpetuating.

Instead of blaming your apparent shortcomings on your extreme old age, can you:

- tell yourself that forgetting something was a one-off lapse of concentration?
- look for the real reason why you are finding an activity difficult? (Tiredness? stress? lack of motivation?)
- say that next time you attempt this particular task, your memory or your skill level will be fine – maybe even better than before?
- gain inspiration from the numerous people throughout history (and people you know or read about in the papers) who have done amazing things when they are over the age of 70?
- look for techniques that will help you make best use of your memory and other abilities? (Mind Maps are one)

If neurons were to die ...
This part is for all those cynics out there who want to cling onto the belief that they are losing about 1,000 brain cells a day. Even if this were true, by the time you were 80 you would have lost $1,000 \times 365 \times 80$ neurons = about 29. 2 million neurons. This is less than 1 per cent of the total number available to you (remember that this total is approximately 10 billion).

The myth may have grown up because neurons do not regenerate, although most cells in the human body are able to do so. The reason for this is that our brain cells don't have to reproduce themselves – we all have far more than we can use in one lifetime anyway! The neurons you are born with are the same ones you have throughout your life, and they are with you when you die.

The only people who do lose brain cells are the unfortunate victims of accidents or strokes. Because the neurons do not regenerate, you might think that such people would be mentally and physically handicapped by such events for the rest of their lives. However, many of them have astounded their doctors by relearning the skills of walking, talking, reading, using their limbs and so on. In some cases, the concentrated focus on improvement has made the people concerned mentally and physically better than before.

Making associations

Every word, idea, image, taste, touch or smell that pops into your brain triggers off a pathway of associations connecting it with other words, ideas and images. This is why one thing reminds you of another (how, say, that farmyard smell reminds you of childhood holidays), how we are able to put ideas together to write this book, and how human beings are capable of brilliant innovative thought.

Have you noticed how sometimes you remember something that you thought you had forgotten? This is because a piece of data entering your brain has triggered off a trail of connections that took you back to that idea. Are you sometimes surprised when you have some insight that has never dawned on you before? This happens when you are able to connect some new information with something that you have known for some time – to relate, indeed, what might be two quite different pieces of information.

When your brain is presented with an idea, a smell, a taste, an image and so on, it is capable of making tens, hundreds or tens of thousands of connections. These are unique to you because they are based on your own life experiences and perceptions. As an example, we have made a 'flow' of connections with the word 'mountain' – see the diagram.

Figure 8   *A flow of connections for the word 'mountain'*

Activity

Now try making your own flow of connections with the word 'money'. Write nine connected words on lines as shown in the above-mentioned diagram. Don't puzzle too long about this.

Now ask a colleague or a friend to do the same thing. It is extremely unlikely that the person will end up with exactly the same words as you: he or she will probably have only one or two of the same words in his/her list.

Activity

This activity is also about associations: this time it's the 'bloom' of associations, and you will be creating a simplified version of a Mind Map.

Write 10 words that you associate with the word 'family' on the 10 lines that radiate out from it. Don't puzzle too long about this: do it as quickly as possible.

If possible, ask at least one other person to do the same activity. Once again, you will find that you have only one or two of these words in common.

This activity is a much more effective brainstorm than the normal linear variety. It is more flexible, and you can see connections between things much more easily than when words are in a vertical list.

By the way, if you think you have a poor memory, it's probably because you are not using it as nature intended. It is much harder to remember isolated facts – easier if they are linked onto other things. We will be discussing memory later in this book.

Summary

Today, you've found out more about the way your brain works. This basis of understanding will help as you go about developing Mind Mapping expertise in more detail.

Creating Mind Maps®

Today – at last – you are going to study Mind Maps in more detail. You will look at how they are constructed and at how this structure makes them infinitely more valuable than other forms of note-making. Throughout the day's period of study, there will also be opportunities for you to practice Mind Mapping yourself.

Reading a Mind Map

The best way to start learning how to construct a Mind Map is to study ones that other people have created. It is important to be aware that some people find them offputting at first. This is simply because they are not used to seeing things noted in this way – particularly in business and education circles. Finding your way around other people's Mind Maps will give you plenty of ideas on how to construct your own. You will soon learn to use a variety of techniques for making your personal creations more attractive and more effective.

Look at the diagram of the 'New starter' Mind Map for a few seconds and then read the explanation underneath.

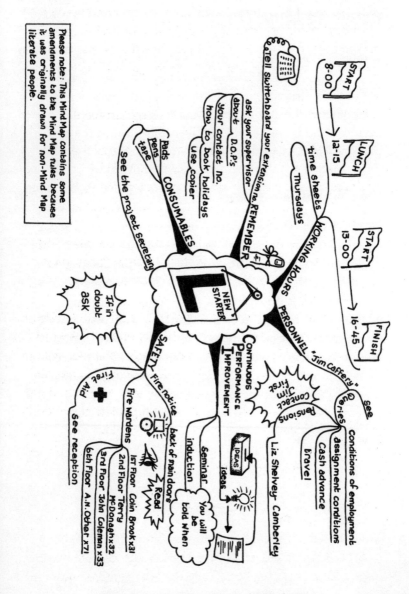

Figure 9 *A 'New Starter' Mind Map*

On this Mind Map, ideas are shown as coloured images and key words as branching out from a central theme. One of the great benefits of Mind Maps like this is that they help you to see how ideas link to each other as well as how they relate to the central theme.

This is how the above Mind Map was constructed:

1 The creator started with a coloured image of the core subject in the centre – a picture and/or words representing the topic on which she wanted to focus her thoughts. In this case, she was thinking about all the things new recruits need.
2 She then let her mind flow freely around this idea and image. First she printed the main themes ('personnel', 'working hours' and so on) on thick curved lines connected to the central topic.
3 Then she added a second level of thought with words or images connected to the main branches that triggered them. Under consumables, for example, she has written 'pads', 'pens' and 'tape', and under 'safety' she has 'fire', 'wardens' and 'first aid'. These lines are thinner than the main branches, and words are again printed along them.
4 The Mind Mapper continued to add third and fourth levels as the thoughts came to her, using images as much as she could.

The rules of Mind Mapping

It may seem a contradiction to say that you have to obey rules when you are producing Mind Maps. But the nature of the rules is crucial here. They are not negative ones which constrain and limit – they are by contrast positive, supportive and therefore liberating.

The whole point of the rules is to provide a structure within which you will have the confidence to explore and develop your ideas. The best Mind Maps are the ones that live by the 'loose–tight' principle. On the one hand, they are rigidly controlled by a number of tried and tested rules, and on the other they allow maximum creativity and individual expression.

Remember that the mind is like a computer that works best when it is correctly programmed and focused. The strict framework of Mind Mapping rules is the channel which will enable you to explore parts of your mind that you would never normally be able to access.

Ten basic Mind Mapping rules are set out below:

1 Place the paper in a landscape position. 'Landscape' simply means positioning the long side of the paper so that it is at the top. This horizontal orientation makes the Mind Map easier to look at because your eyes are set side by side, not one above the other! You will also find that you can fit more information on the page when the paper is in this position.

2 Start with a coloured image in the centre. The image that you start with is crucial to the success of the Mind Map. This central image represents the idea or question that you are going to explore or answer, so it's worth spending a few minutes clarifying it and getting it right before moving on.

   – Make the image between three and five centimetres high and the same width.
   – Do not put a frame around your image: allow it to have its own unique shape.

   If you find it hard to draw an image at first, try using a word or two to represent the topic of your Mind Map. You can always make these words more expressive and attractive by incorporating pictures or patterns into the letters and using three or more colours.

3 Draw the main themes of the Mind Map on thick branches radiating out from the central image. For example, if the topic of the Mind Map is the business planning process, the main themes might be objectives, marketing, resources, personnel and monitoring. If you are using words rather than

pictures, print them along the branches as shown
in the first 'Business Planning' Mind Map diagram.

Figure 10 *An initial 'Business Planning' Mind Map*

4 Use lines to link second and third levels of pictures
   or words to the main branches. Each idea or image
   is further broken down into further levels which flow
   or radiate from the previous ones. See the second
   'Business Planning' Mind Map diagram.

Figure 11 *A developed 'Business Planning' Mind Map*

5 Use images throughout your Mind Map.
   Remember, images stimulate your right brain,
   attract the eye and stimulate your memory. You can
   use patterns, shapes and symbols as well as stick
   figures and tiny pictures. Use images either instead
   of or as well as words on your Mind Map.

6 Print key words. For reading-back purposes, a
   printed word is clearer, more legible and easier to
   remember than ordinary handwriting. The little
   extra time that it takes you to print will be
   compensated for in the time you save when
   reviewing your Mind Map.

7 Put the printed words on lines. You must write or
   draw words or pictures on the lines, and each line
   should be connected to other lines. This
   guarantees that the Mind Map holds together and
   that it has a recognisable shape and structure.

8 Put only one word on each line. This leaves each
   word more free hooks and gives note-taking more
   freedom and flexibility.

9 Make your lines curved and organic. The Mind Map
   is a growing structure that mirrors the way that
   many living things develop. Furthermore, curved
   lines are more attractive and more pleasant to
   draw than straight ones, and they will add to the
   pleasure of creating and reviewing it.

10 Use colours throughout the Mind Map. As we have
   seen, colours enhance memory, delight the eye
   and stimulate the right-brain processes. We shall
   discuss the use of colours on Mind Maps a little
   later in the section.

Because of the large amount of association involved in
Mind Maps, they can be very creative: they tend to
generate new ideas and links that you had never thought of
before. Every item in a Mind Map is in effect the centre of
another map, and if you had time, you could go on
generating Mind Maps for ever!

Activities

Imagine that it is Wednesday and you are doing a
Mind Map in the early morning to help you remember
all the things that you have to do today. The Mind Map
shown already includes two main theme branches.
Add two more and then go on to include second and
third levels of thought, either where we have drawn
lines or on your own lines.

Figure 12 *A partially completed Mind Map*

When you have worked on this Mind Map for a few
minutes, check through the 10 rules described above
to see whether you were able to put them into
practice. Don't worry if you haven't been able to
observe them all – few can at first! Just make a
mental note of which ones you forgot and resolve to
try to follow them next time.

Then, on a separate piece of plain A4 paper, do your own Mind Map using colours and pictures and bearing in mind all you have learned today. Use any theme you like for this – it's best if you focus on something that you can relate to. If you are short of ideas, try this one just to practise:

Imagine that you are going to be asked to do a five-minute presentation to introduce yourself to a group of managers at a conference. Create a Mind Map as an aide memoire for your presentation. Use the following main themes, and move on from there:

- work
- ambitions
- family
- leisure
- interests

Try not to slow down the process by thinking too much about where things should go or whether they should be included. The idea is to recall everything your mind thinks of around the central idea. As your mind will generate ideas faster than you can write, there should be almost no pause – if you do pause, you will probably notice your pen or pencil dithering over the page. The moment you notice this, get it back down and carry on. Do not worry about order or organisation as this will in many cases take care of itself. If it does not, a final ordering can be completed at the end of the exercise.

Your questions answered

Here are some of the many questions that people ask when they are starting to do Mind Maps for the first time. Are yours here?

1 How do I use colour on the Mind Map?
You can use colour to make things stand out, to group things together or simply to make your Mind Map look more attractive. Here are some more specific ideas that other people have found useful and appealing:

- Colour-code the main branches or themes. For example, the red branch and twigs are about the telephone calls I have to make. The blue is about meetings I have to attend. The green represents letters I have to write. I might even take a purple pen to highlight the most urgent tasks and a brown one to mark the ones that may safely be left till tomorrow.
- Use one colour for the thickest lines nearest to the central theme. Use another colour for second-level thoughts and others for the third and fourth and so on.
- Use colours to represent different people's contributions to a group Mind Map. Susan is using a blue pen, Ross writes and draws in red, and Leonie does her mapping in green.
- Use one strong colour for all the main branches and the lines. Then use other colours to write key words and sketch pictures. You can apply colours as they appear in nature (green trees, blue sea etc.) or try a more surreal approach (purple hair, pink clouds etc.)

It all comes down to the fact that you can apply colour in any way that you like. And even if you find a way that works for you, don't get stuck in a rut. You will never know the value of a particular approach until you actually try it.

2 What if I can't draw?

You already know the answer to this one if you read through Monday's material. For a start, drawing is a skill that you can learn just like any other, if you want to. But you don't have to be a Rembrandt or a Matisse to create effective Mind Maps – many people manage very well with simple shapes and patterns. Don't worry too much about drawing – just do the best you can. As you become more involved in Mind Mapping, you will notice more aspects of the world around you: shapes, colours, contrasts and perspectives. Your drawing will automatically improve as you start to see things with the eye of an artist, and in turn your creative abilities and other mental functions will improve as well.

3 What do I do if I make a mistake?
   There's no such thing as a mistake! Mind Maps are
   never wrong, they are simply the product of your logical
   and imagistic brain. What may seem like a mistake at
   first may in fact be some fantastic insight that has never
   occurred to you before.
   If you want to change or edit your Mind Map, you can
   always:

   – use correcting fluid
   – stick a piece of paper over the part you want to change
   – use the correct width of tape
   – sketch out the Mind Map in pencil to get the
     structure and main themes right before applying
     any ink or colour
   – use a Mind Mapping software program
   – start again, using your original effort as a 'first draft'

4 How do I know when my Mind Map is finished?
   A Mind Map is never finished! You simply decide that it has
   fulfilled its purpose or that the time or paper is used up!

   In fact, one of the dangers is that you may become so
   engrossed that you spend far longer on one than you
   originally intended. If this is a problem for you, decide how
   long you want to spend on a Mind Map and set a timer to
   go off when that limit is up. If at that stage you are exploring
   some interesting ideas, you can always decide to extend
   the allotted period. If, however, you do have to leave the
   Mind Map to get on with something else, you will find that it
   is quite easy to come back to it a few hours or even days
   later.

The word is the key ...

Another question that people often ask is how to select the right key words to place on the main branches and lines of the Mind Map. The answer is, once again, that the 'right' key words are just ones that encapsulate an idea and trigger off the desired associations.

Key words tend to be the nouns (names of things or people) and verbs (run, write, cook) in a sentence. However, sometimes you may want to use adjectives (big, beautiful), adverbs (quickly, effectively) or even pronouns (me, you, he, they). You will not need to use prepositions (in, on) and conjunctions (with, and).

About 90 per cent of the words you write down during traditional forms of note-taking are not really needed. The redundant articles are the abstract words of little substance that serve to glue sentences together and make pieces of prose flow freely. When you are reading your long-winded linear notes, your eyes will not even stop to look at these superfluous words, because most of the meaning of a sentence or a paragraph is conveyed by the *key* words.

Activity

Underline the key words in the following extract:

The traditional Swiss watch industry was decimated in the early 1980s by imports of cheap digital watches from Asia. However, Swiss marketing research revealed that many people would like to use watches with different colours and designs as a fashion accessory. This is how the Swatch was born – and it revitalised the whole industry.

The words that are the most memorable and contain the essence of the passage's meaning are *Swiss watch industry, decimated, digital, Asia, research, fashion accessory, Swatch, revitalised*. The diagram shows how those key words might be presented in Mind Map form.

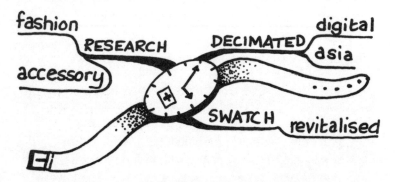

Figure 13 *A Mind Map on the Swiss watch industry*

By identifying key words or ideas and placing them
appropriately on a Mind Map, you are also:

- imposing a form of organisation on the material
- allowing associations and interpretations to emerge
- drawing attention to what is important
- integrating the new material with what you know already

All these benefits will help you to recall your notes later –
with greater clarity and in more detail than you would
have been able to achieve with traditional forms of notes.

Key words also tend to be:

- concrete rather than abstract
- capable of generating 'thought pictures'
- capable of triggering other ideas and key words
- easily recalled

Many people find that the simple act of finding the word
that expresses what they want to say – the one that forms
the nub of an idea they want to analyse – in itself clarifies
their thoughts and opens up whole new avenues to explore
and develop. Find the appropriate key word and you will
know what you think, feel, remember or believe.

Benefits of Mind Mapping

You will find it useful to finish today's section by trying to
summarise how Mind Maps represent a more effective
approach to note-making than other more traditional
methods.

> ### Activity
>
> Think about the Mind Maps that you have done so far and suggest three advantages over the linear form of note-taking.

In the above activity, you will have noted points that are more obvious or important to you. Did your ideas include any of these?

- you can get a lot of information on one piece of paper
- the relative importance of each idea is clearly indicated. More important ideas are near the centre and the supporting details are near the edge
- the links between the key concepts are immediately recognisable because of their proximity and connection
- the structure and nature of the Mind Map makes review and recall more effective and more rapid
- you can easily add new information without messy scratching out or squeezing in
- every Map made will look and be different from every other Mind Map. This will aid recall
- because the Mind Map is open-ended, the brain is able to make new connections – suddenly you can tap into your creative abilities
- because Mind Mapping is fun, you will find that you are keen to undertake tasks that may have seemed daunting in the past. You may suddenly be able to tackle that project, do your business plan or write a speech
- Mind Maps are simple to create once you get used to them – and they have many different uses. You will be looking in more detail at these different uses on Friday of this week

Summary

Today you have studied Mind Maps in more detail, learning how to create one for yourself and considering some common questions about them. You have also looked at how they can offer a more effective approach to a routine activity like taking notes than the conventional linear style.

On the tip of your tongue

How often have you heard someone say 'Oh I have a memory like a sieve' or 'She has the memory of a goldfish'?

If our experience is anything to go by, then probably quite often. However, the reality is that each of us has an infinite capacity to remember – but not everyone knows they do.

When you remember things, you are forming new associations with known points on an existing network. You are using familiar ideas to understand new concepts.

Why is memory important?

A lot of people underestimate the importance of memory – 'Why do I need to know X's phone number, or Y's email address, when I can make a note on a post-it, or in my electronic diary?'

However, memory is much more than facts and figures – it is an important part of your make up. If you had no memory, you would never have learned to walk, talk, read, write or dress yourself. How would you find your way home every night without memory? Or remember to set the video for your favourite show each day? The simple answer is that you wouldn't.

And whats more, you would not be able to recall anything we have just said about memory!

Every single action you perform, every idea you have, every conscious or unconscious thought is a function of your memory.

The tiny percentage of things you might forget in a day pales into insignificance compared to everything you remember. They would appear as a few flakes of snow on the white carpet of the alps. And the good news is that we have already learned enough about our brains to help improve our memory.

It may not be a life-long ambition to recite every Grand National winner since the war, but it would be nice to remember the name of the horse you got in the sweep at work. You might consider it unnecessary to know the mobile phone number for every single one of your clients, but surely it would be a bonus to know your own!

It would also be good to be able to call to mind:

- the key points of a presentation without needing to bury yourself in the notes
- how to find that crucial file that you know you saved somewhere on the system

- the names of all your customers and how they take their coffee

If you find yourself becoming enthusiastic about memory techniques, you may find yourself memorising all kinds of things that you never dreamed possible: events that happened months or even years ago, your own dreams, pieces from newspapers or books and the things people have said to you.

Feats of memory

There are countless remarkable examples of the human brain's capacity to remember, and in one such notable example in the early twentieth century, psychologists found that a Russian journalist called Sheresehevsky ('S') had a perfect memory. He could remember everything, without ever taking notes. After 30 years of research, it was concluded that, although S had a normal brain there was apparently no limit to his capacity to remember. He had never been taught techniques of memory: he was a natural *synaesthetist* (i.e. natural at blending the senses).

The memory is not like a receptacle that eventually becomes so full that there is no room left for any more memories. Rather, it is a tree that thrives as memories accumulate and nourish it. Each new idea acts like a twig on which more memories can be hung – so the more you know, the more you are able to know.

Memory and memory techniques are fascinating and rewarding subjects which we don't have space to discuss in great detail here. However, if you do want to study the memory systems that people use to perform the above feats, you could start by selecting one or two books from the reading list on page 96.

Why do we forget?

If the brain has an almost infinite capacity to remember, why is it that we seem to forget things so easily? Here are four reasons why we forget:

1 *repression* – forgetting things that are unpleasant or painful
2 *mindset* – believing that the memory is poor
3 *absentmindedness* – concentrating on the wrong thing
4 *interference* – too many similar memories become mixed up

Repression
Freud famously hypothesised that we unconsciously repress memories that cause us pain or anxiety. You probably find it more difficult to remember the negative things about your childhood than those aspects that you found pleasant and enjoyable. Sometimes, memories are so repressed that they can only be accessed when a person undergoes hypnosis. For most people, however, it is possible that repression explains only a small proportion of our forgetfulness.

The important point is that if you want to remember things better, you must associate them with something positive, pleasant or fun. Later in this section, you will see how these kinds of associations can be made.

Mindset
Mindset refers to your state of mind, your attitudes and your beliefs about yourself and the world. Remember, the

brain, like any other computer, responds to its programming – that is, to the questions you ask it, the challenges you set and the images it perceives.

It may help to know that World Memory Champion Dominic O'Brien did not start life as a person noted for having a phenomenal memory. However, he became interested when he watched a memory expert perform on TV, and decided to see if he could do the same himself. He was not very successful at first but persisted because he was highly motivated and because he believed he would achieve his goals in the end. Eight years after he had first started, he had been World Memory Champion three times and had achieved numerous astounding memory feats, including memorising 35 packs of cards in 13 hours.

We're not saying that you should set yourself such challenges, but simply that if you believe you can improve your memory and you want to do so, you will.

Absentmindedness
This means that your mind is elsewhere when it should be concentrating on its object – listening to someone speak, remembering a face, taking note of where you are putting the car keys or reading a book.

A lot of 'forgetting' is not really forgetting at all – it is failing to lodge things properly in the brain in the first place. To remember things, you have to make a definite memory trace – a hook that will help you to recall the fact, the face, the name or the idea the next time you need it.

An important step to a better memory is therefore to resolve to take notice of what is going on around you, to

observe people, to listen to what they are saying and to be aware of what you yourself are doing.

Interference

Interference – as Peter Russell calls it in *The Brain Book* – is probably the most common reason for forgetting. This theory suggests that forgetting occurs because the required memory cannot be distinguished from other similar memory traces. The memories literally interfere with one another. It is impossible, for example, to remember what you had for lunch on one particular Friday in 1997 because the memories of all those similar lunches become mixed up over a period of time. The problem is not that you have too many memories, because the brain has an infinite capacity to remember. The problem is rather that you don't have enough cues to enable you to distinguish one lunch from all the others.

The kinds of cues that may help you to recall that particular lunch could be:

- the fact that it was your birthday that same day

(remembering this fact might trigger the other associated
memory)
*   eating something that you have never eaten before or
    since (tasting or seeing that food again could bring the
    memory back)
*   the outfit that you wore that day (seeing those same
    clothes hanging in the wardrobe or putting them on could
    bring the memory of the lunch flooding back)

Too often, we have to wait for the right association to help
us to remember things. You must have experienced those
annoying times when the required memory pops up three
days later than it is actually required. The trick is to take
control, to ensure that important memories have strong
associations so that they can be recalled when they are
needed – not when it suits them to make an appearance.

Mind Maps and mnemonics

The word we use to describe memory techniques is
mnemonics – a name derived from the Greek goddess of
memory, Mnemosyne. One mnemonic most of us are
familiar with is '30 days hath September, April, June and
November …' and so on. The point is that using memory
techniques is not cheating: if you want to recall anything, it
is simply not possible to remember it in isolation. You have
to link it to something that is already fixed inside your
brain. The fixed item is the 'hook' on which the newly
acquired memory will hang. A Mind Map can incorporate a
number of hooks to aid recall: images, symbols, patterns,
colour, emphasis, humour, texture, dimensions, logical
structure, sequence, senses and so on. The more
imaginative you are as you create your Mind Maps, the

better the associations will be and the easier it will be to remember them.

We have already discussed many of the above points, but here are a few additional ways in which you can make your Mind Maps more memorable:

- *add humour.* Give your imagination a free rein when you create your Mind Maps – the funnier and more absurd they are, the easier they will be to remember
- *exaggerate.* The process of emphasis will assist your memory. Make important words or parts of words stand out by making them big. Give certain images more prominence by making them larger than life
- *add dimensions.* You can use boxes, shading, shadows, perspectives, spirals and dots to make your Mind Maps – or parts of them – stand out from the page and help you to remember them
- *include 'sensitising' images.* You can use, for example:
  - colourful pictures that suggest tastes and smells

- spikes, dots, bumps and so on to give texture
- word 'tags' to suggest different noises – see the diagram

Figure 14 *Word 'tags' as a Mind Map to suggest different noises*

- *outline the shape of a branch.* putting borders round the main branches and their offshoots provides you with a memorable shape that you can then associate with that chapter heading or that theme. You can make your borders look like clouds, steps, splats, ink blots, chains, scribbles – anything that relates to the subject of the branch, or that makes it more memorable for you; see the diagram

Figure 15 *A Mind Map with an outline around a branch*

Activity

Try using a Mind Map to plan a presentation, a contribution to a meeting or an important phone call. Use as many of the above features as possible, having two or three goes if you are not happy about your first efforts.

Review the Mind Map carefully a few minutes after you have completed it. Then, half an hour later, see how many points you can remember without looking back at the Mind Map.

The importance of review

Review is vital for memory because otherwise you are spending a lot of time collecting information and then allowing it to fade away. You will find it impossible to build up a solid basis of knowledge because you constantly have to put the same items into your brain over and over again. It becomes difficult to move on, to acquire new information and to use what you already know creatively. If, on the other hand, you do invest time in reviewing things that are important to you, you will create a rich store of facts, concepts, ideas and theories which you can draw on and add to as and when you need them. You will also find that, the more you know, the easier it is to secure new knowledge.

How to review
Research shows that our memory is at its best a few minutes after a period of study or reading. It is thought that this happens because during those minutes the brain is subconsciously integrating the new data with what it already knows and making new associations. The bad news is that during the next 24 hours, we then lose 80 per cent of the detail of what we learned during that period!

The graph shown illustrates what normally happens after you have studied, read or learned something.

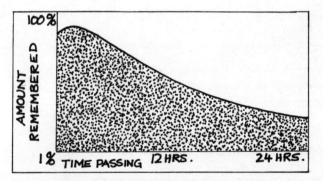

Figure 16 *A memory rhythm graph*

To lodge things in the long-term memory, it is therefore important to make the most of the high points and to make sure that the low points never happen. You should try to get into the habit of:

- making a Mind Map summary of the topic
- doing a quick review 10 minutes after you have finished looking at something new. This will consolidate what you have learned at the time when recall is at its highest point
- spending a few minutes reviewing that same information 24 hours later. This will start to lodge it in your long-term memory
- doing a third review one week later
- doing a fourth review one month later

During this month, you will, of course, have been acquiring more information which you will link in with what you have already learned. Making these new associations will give you fresh insights and will help you to keep a mental hold on the key points that you want to retain.

Taking notes from written material

A lot of people find that one of the best uses they have for Mind Mapping is to help recall the key points from written material.

Activity

Try Mind Mapping a book you have read recently or are reading at the moment. Make sure that you select a book that contains information or ideas that you want to remember.

1 Use the title or subject of the book for your central image and the chapter headings for your main branches.

2 Note down only the main ideas in the form of words and pictures – if you do any more, the Mind Map will become too complicated. If you have really understood the book, the key words and images will trigger the rest of the information for you.

3 Review your Mind Map after 10 minutes, one day later, one week later and one month later. Do this each time by sketching out the Mind Map from memory and comparing it with your original one. (This need only take a few minutes of your time.)

4 After one month, create a new Mind Map that incorporates all the features of the first one and any new ideas that have since occurred to you or any knowledge that you have collected in the meantime.

The key points of the book will now be in your long-term memory, and you will have made the information your own.

Summary

Today we have considered the human memory, including outstanding memory feats, the use of mnemonics and, at the other end of the spectrum, the reasons for poor memory performance. We have then looked at Mind Mapping as a way of pepping up your memory.

Mind Maps® for ... just about everything

You can use Mind Maps in almost every set of circumstances where you would normally write linear notes or jot down lists of words. The more you use Mind Maps, the more uses will suggest themselves to you. Today, we have included some of the main ones just to get you started.

Decision-making

Mind Mapping can be of tremendous value when you are trying to make a decision. Many of our decisions are made and acted on in a split second – sometimes the process takes place so fast that we are hardly aware that we have actually made a decision. But it's important to analyse what is happening and how the process can be improved because:

- your decisions are the means by which you move your work on to achieve your tasks and goals, and

- the way in which you make decisions can determine the extent to which others are committed to the content of those decisions

Activity

List three important decisions you have made during the past month.

1

2

3

When you make a decision, you are at a crossroads: having to select one option out of two or more options. As a manager, you have to make many different kinds of decisions – if you think about it, you will realise that you are making them virtually all the time. Some are to do with your day-to-day operation; others are more long-term and strategic in nature.

Next time you have to make an important decision, try using the main branches of a Mind Map to identify the different options available and to explore the implications of each one. The process of free association around the alternative options will enable you to think deeply about them and, in some cases, to clarify your personal feelings.

If a single Mind Map does not allow enough space to examine the different ideas in enough detail, you could make your preferred options the topic of individual Mind Maps.

Some of the advantages of using Mind Mapping rather than 'logical' decision-making processes are:

- you may come up with ideas that you never thought of before. This happens because you will be using both your imaginative right brain and your logical left brain, heightening your creative *whole* brain
- you may be able to think radiantly (in all directions) as you become more relaxed. This means looking at a problem or a decision from a different point of view. It is important to allow the 'wacky' ideas to come as well as the more sensible ones: some of the greatest decisions and inventions in history have been developed from the strangest of beginnings
- you can actually start to develop your ideas to see what they may involve. This process of exploration will help you to decide how you feel about the different options. It could also trigger new ideas
- you can see how different ideas relate to each other. This may help you to combine two or more of them in the option you finally select

You may find, as many people do, that the very act of Mind Mapping actually helps you to identify the decision you want to make or recommend to others.

You can also use Mind Maps if the issue simply involves deciding between two obvious courses of action. The example shown in the diagram, created by Vanda North, Director of Buzan Centres Ltd, has been used to analyse the pros and cons of moving to new premises. Notice that Vanda has weighted each key word by giving it a number from 1 to 100. This was also done by the team members. Finally, she added the scores up to find out which one had the highest total.

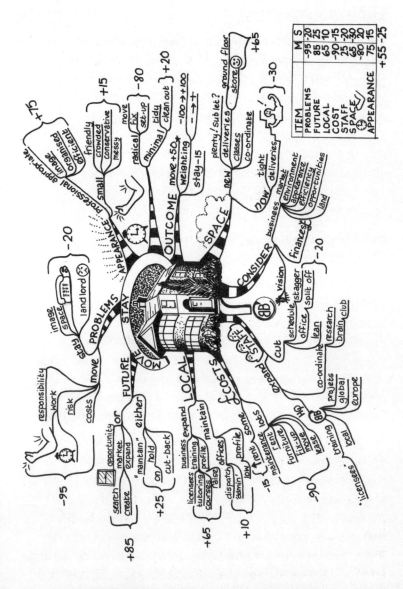

Figure 17 A 'Move or Stay' Mind Map

Time management

Time is potentially as precious as any other resource you might have at your disposal. And yet most of us would probably admit that we can manage and use our time more effectively. Mind Maps can help us to make the most of our times by establishing our priorities and allocating our time accordingly. If you can master this skill, you will be able to stay in control of situations, even when you are suddenly hit by the unexpected. You can also enjoy your free time, safe in the knowledge that you have left plenty of opportunity to get everything done.

Mind Maps can help us to manage our time in many ways – here are three we have picked out:

Your long- and short-term goals
Whether you are looking six months into the future, or two years, you will want to establish goals. These give you your direction and help you prioritise what needs doing, and when. Mind Maps can help determine how long each step will take, what you will need to do for each and when they need to be done by. You can then see if you can save time by combining two steps that overlap, or keeping apart two steps that might conflict with each other.

Things to do
A lot of people find that making a list of 'things to do' helps them to focus on what needs to be done during a particular day, week or period of weeks. You might find that you can save time and make these lists more effective, if you put them into a Mind Map format. It is worth getting into the habit of making your lists at the same time each day – maybe last thing at night, or first thing in the

morning. This will get you into a routine, which can save time and ensure that you maximise every available minute you have. Once you have made your list, you will have to decide:

- in what order you will tackle the items you have to do
- how long you will spend on each one

There are several advantages to planning your day or your week in Mind Map form:

- it gives you the chance to think through each task – you may even begin to imagine yourself doing them and to visualise the desired outcomes. This can make even the most daunting tasks seem less unpleasant – good news for procrastinators!
- the Mind Map helps to commit your tasks to memory. You will find that you can fit things into little 'windows' of time that appear unexpectedly during

the day, that you are less likely to forget to do
things, and that very little time is wasted
• if you do have to fit other unexpected requirements
into your day, you can return to your original time
plan when the other matters have been dealt with.
You will find it a relatively easy to task to replan the
remainder of the day's activities on the basis of a
quick reassessment of your priorities and goals

A Mind Map diary
As you become more used to the approaches that we are
describing, you may like to investigate the uses and value
of the 'Universal Personal Organiser'. This is a life-
planning system developed by Tony Buzan and described
in detail in *The Mind Map Book*. As well as the verbal, linear
and logical skills used in conventional diaries, the Mind
Map diary incorporates colour, pictures, symbols, humour
and so on.

This system allows you to make:

• *a yearly plan* – giving you an overview of the major
events for the whole year
• *a monthly plan* – this is an expansion of the yearly
plan, showing major events in more detail
• *a daily plan* – this is based on the 24-hour clock,
with events noted in their time slots using colour
codes, pictures, symbols and key words

This approach to life management will help you to get the
whole of your time in balance – so that you are allocating it
in ways that are important for you.

Making lists

'To do' lists are probably only one of many types of lists that people make both at work and during their personal lives. Most of us make lists at one time or another – either to plan some future event or to help us to remember things.

> ### Activity
>
> Make a note of three kinds of lists that you make.

Some people are compulsive list-makers – we've even heard of people who make lists of their lists to help them keep track of things! Any or all of the following types of lists can be converted into Mind Map form. We've done this in the form of a mini Mind Map, just to prove that we are not obsessive about lists! See the diagram.

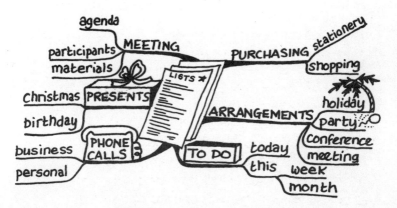

Figure 18   *A mini list Mind Map*

- purchasing – stationery, shopping
- arrangements – holiday, party, conference, meeting
- to do – today, this week, this month
- meeting – participants, agenda, materials
- presents – Christmas, birthday
- phone calls – business, personal

You can produce your lists in different ways to suit the particular circumstances or your own perspective on the situation. For instance, the shopping list is most likely to be broken down in terms of:

- fruit
- vegetables
- dairy
- drinks
- and so on

However, it might suit you to list your shopping under different subheadings, for example:

- basics
- nice to have
- treats

or

- supermarket
- craft shop
- clothes shop

or

- main meals
- packed lunches
- party food

The possibilities are infinite, as you will find when you become more experienced in Mind Mapping.

Activity

Make a 'to do' list or some other form of list and then convert it into Mind Map form. Compare the two forms of making notes, and consider the benefits of the Mind Map.

Taking notes during meetings, presentations, lectures or speeches

This is one of the most valuable uses for Mind Maps. Some people feel it is also one of the most difficult types because you are creating the Mind Map while other people are speaking – and unfortunately, you can't rewind the tape if you happen to miss something! However, as is often the case with skills that are a bit tricky to master, the reward that you will gain from being able to do this type of Mind Mapping makes it well worth the effort of persevering. This is because you are not only making a record of what is being said, you are also organising the information in a way that will make it easy to remember, integrating it with the things you already know and adding your own comments and reactions as you go along.

When you are Mind Mapping from the spoken word, get your central image from the topic of the meeting, speech or presentation. This image should be strong enough to take your mind right back to the meeting when you review your notes – so make it as colourful, humorous and exaggerated as possible. You may be able to prepare your main branches from the meeting agenda or any printed materials provided by the speaker. If this is not possible, you will have to listen hard to work out what the main themes are as you go along. Good speakers will help their audiences to follow what they are saying by telling them in advance what they are going to cover and then doing a quick resumé at the end.

Don't worry too much, however, if your Mind Mapped notes end up looking messy and disorganised. They will still probably be 10 times as good as pages and pages of linear notes. If it is very important to have a clear record of the event, you can always do a neat copy later by way of review.

In the book *Get Ahead*, Vanda North makes a number of suggestions for making sure that you don't miss anything when you are taking notes from the spoken word:

- start with a low-risk activity. For example, you can practise Mind Mapping the news or a speech which you don't have to remember in great detail
- create a Mind Map from your linear notes – this is a good way of reviewing the main points of a lecture and making sure that you will be able to remember the main points

- work with a 'buddy' – one of you producing a hand-written record of the event and the other one creating a Mind Map – and then compare notes
- use a small tape recorder and mark down the number that appears on the tape counter at the places where you lost track or missed some important points

Taking notes from written material

This topic was largely covered yesterday. The technique is very similar to taking notes from the spoken word except that it is a lot easier because you have more time to think.

You can either use the chapter headings or subheadings of a report for your main branches or look for particular points of your own. If you are Mind Mapping a novel, for instance, the areas that you are looking for may include:

- plot
- characters
- setting
- themes
- author

Planning written material

Any kind of written material can be prepared using Mind Maps – letters, memos, reports, books. What happens is that you do all your thinking before you actually start writing rather than during the process of writing. The result is that you can develop all your ideas and see where they relate to each other before committing them to paper.

Instead, your finished product will be focused and concise, you will waste little time in revising and editing, and the piece of text should be easy for others to read.

Planning presentations

Any speeches, presentations or training sessions that you are involved in will benefit from your spending time preparing them in Mind Map form. There are many advantages to using this method of preparation:

- it is much easier to memorise your presentation when it is on a single piece of paper with all the Mind Map features (ideas clustered around the main theme, pictures, key words, symbols, colours and so on)

- you will not have to keep referring to lengthy notes written on paper or cards (there is therefore less risk that you will lose your place, or that the audience will lose track of what you are saying)
- because you do not have to read from written notes, you will be able to maintain eye contact with the audience. Furthermore, your presentation will be natural and relaxed, rather than stilted and formal
- you will be able to maintain the structure and the focus of the presentation even if questions or comments from your listeners force you to stray off the point temporarily

In short, a Mind Mapped presentation allows you to be flexible and informal while at the same time maintaining the required structure and clarity. The net result is that you will feel confident and relaxed while giving a presentation, and you will be able to communicate effectively with your audience.

Group Mind Maps

One final point before we finish today's material is that most of the Mind Maps we have been discussing today can be created by a group as well as by individuals. This is well worth the experiment because, if you remember how many brain cells there are in one brain alone, think of how many brain cells are involved if three or more people produce a Mind Map as a joint effort! There are many prerequisites for an effective group Mind Map, including healthy open relationships between the people involved and a willingness to listen to each others' ideas.

It is a good idea for the group members to do an individual 'brain bloom' – similar to the family activity on Tuesday – before contributing to a group Mind Map. In this way, individuals will have thought through their personal ideas before the group effort begins. There are many benefits to group Mind Mapping, including:

- all members will feel that they have made a contribution and will therefore be willing to commit themselves to the outcome
- associations will be triggered not only by one's own ideas but also by the ideas of other people in the group. They in turn will be inspired by your ideas and the way you express them
- they are great fun!

Remember again:

- all Mind Maps are 'right' if they achieve your aim. The ones that you have produced will probably be very different from others' on the same subject, and this merely reflects your different perspectives and ideas
- Mind Maps are always open. If you want to, you can make your brain continue to explore the topic by adding extra branches

Summary

Today, you have explored in some detail a diverse range of Mind Maps covering areas like decision-making, time management (including a Mind Map diary technique), list-making and note-taking. You have also looked at the advantages of planning speeches, presentations and training sessions by using Mind Maps.

A work-out for the brain

In this book, we have sought to show that Mind Mapping is itself an excellent work-out for the brain. We hope that you have already had some practical experience of Mind Mapping, because it is impossible to describe the benefits adequately in words.

This final day concerns itself with the future: it looks at just a few things that you can do to develop your 'mental circuitry' still further. You will find that as you become a more efficient Mind Mapper, new doors will begin to open and new ideas for improving your performance and fulfilling your potential will occur to you.

Mental exercise

If there is one thing that we have learned in all our research and experience, it is that you have to use the brain or lose it. The amazing thing is that you don't have to put in much extra effort to obtain rich rewards.

There are many forms of mental exercise that will complement your growing Mind Mapping skills and help to develop your mental capacity. Some examples are:

- chess
- bridge
- backgammon
- crosswords
- playing a musical instrument
- drawing or painting
- meditation

In fact, almost any activity that makes you think and that stretches you in unaccustomed mental directions will have a positive effect in other areas of your life.

Memorising

Memorising is one form of mental exercise that will give your brain a great work-out.

Many memory systems involve using 'pegs' or 'hooks'. The idea is to peg the items you want to remember onto certain images that never change. In the number/shape peg system, for example, the pegs are a set of pictures that resemble the shape of numbers. Pegs for 1 to 5 might therefore be:

1 = a pencil
2 = a swan
3 = a heart
4 = the sail of a ship
5 = a fishing hook

You don't have to use these particular pegs. In fact, it's best if you conjure up your own mental images – ones that you find easy or pleasing. You could use a candle for '1', for example.

Once you have completed the relatively easy task of committing the number pegs to memory, you are ready to use them to help you to remember things. Let us say that you are driving to work and you need to do some shopping on the way home. You can't write anything down, so you memorise the items you want to purchase by associating their images with the already-existing peg pictures. The mental pictures that you make must follow the memory principles that we looked at on Thursday. They must be as exaggerated, absurd, colourful, sensuous and three-dimensional as possible. The more of these features that you can weave into the mental images that you create, the easier it will be to recall the items on your shopping list.

Imagine that the first thing you want to buy is a bottle of red wine. The mind picture that you create could be of you sketching a bottle of red wine with an enormous pencil on a massive piece of paper. The pencil is bright red and it feels hard and shiny in your fingers, and you can smell the soft lead as you draw on the paper. When you have almost completed the drawing, the bottle starts to move by itself – it pours some wine into a glass that is on the table beside the pad of paper. You can hear the unmistakable sound of the dark red liquid being poured out, and you savour the aroma of the wine as you prepare to taste it.

It takes much longer to describe the picture in words than it does for you to make the picture in your mind. With practice, it takes only seconds. Hopefully, you have got the idea and now feel able to make similar associations with the other pegs.

Activity

Just for fun, try making associations for the other number pegs.

2 = a swan: a loaf of French bread
3 = a heart: the ingredients for a salad
4 = the sail of a ship: a wedge of fine cheese
5 = a fishing hook: a bunch of grapes

This is, of course, a very easy example. You can extend it to incorporate up to 10 pegs and highly complex items that would be much more difficult to remember than the ones given here.

Nevertheless, test yourself after half an hour and 8 hours later to see if you can recall the items in the correct order.

To find out about other peg systems, you could refer to Tony Buzan's book *Use Your Memory* (see the reading list at the end of this book).

There are memory systems that have been specially devised to help people remember phone numbers, birthdays and names and faces. If you are interested, you can read about these also in the books we have recommended.

Physical health

Having a healthy body and a well-balanced diet are also invaluable for the effective functioning of the brain. To work well, the brain needs:

- plenty of oxygen: this is only possible if the arteries are clear
- vitamin E: to help brain cells make the best use of the available oxygen
- vitamins B and C: to increase mental alertness
- adequate rest: while you are sleeping or taking a break from work, the body is busy renewing the chemicals that it used up while the brain was active.

It's vital to be aware that the most important element to the health of the brain is oxygen. This means that you must ensure that any exercise that you take is *aerobic*. This term describes any kind of physical activity that expands your body's capacity to deliver oxygen to the brain. (Although we are focusing on the brain here, please note that aerobic exercise is also the key to a healthy *body*.)

Activity

Do a Mind Map that identifies the physical and mental exercises that you can undertake to keep both your mind and your body in excellent condition.

Giving yourself a challenge

Giving yourself a challenge is a good way of jolting yourself out of the armchair and expanding your brain power. Depending what challenge you decide to set yourself, this may also help you to make new friends, improve your health and learn new skills. The brain enjoys a challenge because it's so under-used most of the time. Here are some examples of the kinds of challenges that people we know have set themselves:

- walking to the tops of seven mountains in one day
- trekking through the Himalayas
- riding a bicycle down the bank of the Nile
- learning a foreign language
- writing a book
- doing a PhD
- making some new friends
- learning T'ai Chi

You don't need a lot of money to set yourself a challenge and achieve it. All you need is the courage to decide what you would like to do and then do it.

Studying the people you admire

One final tip for developing your brain power and achieving what you want is to identify the people you admire and find out how their lives have been shaped by their beliefs, their attitudes and their actions. If other people are succeeding at something that you would like to achieve, why struggle to discover the secret of success all by yourself? It's fascinating and it's fun to learn from other people's lives, and you can even learn a lot from their mistakes!

Potential role models are all around you. Your own may be famous people, living or dead, or they may be people you work with, friends, or even members of your own family. You will learn by reading books, watching films and asking questions. And you can make full use of your Mind Mapping skills to note down the aspects of their lives that you would like to learn from.

What now?

The main thing for the future is to make Mind Mapping
one of your key tools for planning, decision-making and
note-making – in fact for all the uses we discussed
yesterday and many more. In time, you will become your
own teacher; you will begin to identify the techniques and
the outcomes that work for you and those that are not quite
so useful. Every Mind Mapper develops his or her own
approach, and you will find that your style develops as you
become more experienced.

Activities

Do a Mind Map review of the points you have gained
from reading through this book day by day. What you
got out of the book will be the things that are
important to you – the points that will be of benefit to
you in your future life and work.

Leonardo da Vinci said that 'everything connects to
everything else'. Aim to do at least one Mind Map a
day from now on and you will understand the full
meaning of this statement. Mind Maps are about
connections.

Summary

You have completed the week, and it is time to put
Mind Mapping into practice. We hope you will enjoy
Mind Mapping and that it will help you to make the most
of your mind.

Suggested further reading

Buzan, Tony and Buzan, Barry (1995) *The Mind Map Book*, London: BBC Books, revised edition.

Buzan, Tony and Keene, Raymond (1996) *The Age Heresy*, London: Ebury Press.

Buzan, Tony (1995) *Use Your Head*, London: BBC Books, revised edition

Buzan, Tony (1995) *Use Your Memory*, London: BBC Books, revised edition

Edwards, Betty (1993) *Drawing on the Right Side of the Brain*, London: HarperCollins

North, Vanda and Buzan, Tony (1991) *Get Ahead*, Poole, Dorset: B. C. Books.

Russell, Peter (1994) *The Brain Book*, London: Routledge, reprinted edition.

For further information on Buzan Centre courses, books, videos, audio tapes and other products, please send for our brochure:

UK Head Office
Buzan Centres Ltd.
54 Parkstone Road
Poole
Dorset
BH15 2PX
Tel: 44 (0)1202 674676
Fax: 44 (0)1202 674776
Email: Info@buzan.co.uk

USA Office
Buzan Centre Inc.
415 Federal Highway
Lake Park
Florida
33403
Tel : 001 (561) 881 0188
Fax: 001 561 845 3210
Email: Buzan000@aol.com